COURAGE ROAD

YOUR GUIDE FROM GRIEF TO HOPE

ISBN: 978-0-692-82773-4 (Paperback Edition)

Cover Design by Elizabeth Mackey
Cover Image by Mike Robinson
Book Design by Naomi Vogel

First Edition First Printing

Printed and Bound in USA

Visit www.CourageRoad.com

With gratitude to the following: Hospice of Santa Barbara - a wonderful organization and the foundation for my book; to all my former clients who took their journey with me and taught me the meaning of Courage. To the brave Lovely Ladies of the Widows' Group and to the dearest members of OLG. Joanne Talbot, you are a very special woman and supervisor. Nina Smith, our work together at County Mental Health taught me so much. Katherine Aaron, my virtual assistant at Time Etc., thank you for always helping me at the drop of a hat. Naomi Vogel - I LOVE the design of my book. And special thanks to Dorothy Wallstein who gave me the confidence to put what I know on paper. I would not have started this project without you.

Dedicated to Rachael and Michael, Allen (Team Possible) and Mashee with all my love. Thank you for your enthusiasm and support in my life.

Mary Ransom's compassion and guidance through the emotional journey of grief was vital to me. Her thoughtful work with Hospice of Santa Barbara's Widows Group was a touchstone to the elusive peace at such a tragic time.

Susan Cochran,
Author of In the Sea of Grief and Love

While reading the words of this book, I was reminded of a very dark time in my life when my husband died. I did not believe I could get through the pain, but Mary gently walked me to a place of hope. Her approach is gentle and practical. I am forever grateful.

Beth Morales,
Jail Chaplin

I got to know Mary Ransom during the five years I served as Executive Director of Hospice of Santa Barbara. At that time we were serving hundreds of people every month who were grieving the loss of a loved one. Whether it was the loss of a spouse, parent, or child, Mary consistently proved herself to be a uniquely gifted grief counselor, and you will see why when you read this book. She is genuinely caring, imminently practical, and consistently wise. She knows how hard the grief journey can be, and she knows how best to help. She's guided countless people down this difficult road towards healing and hope, and with this clear and engaging guidebook, I know she will help countless more. Trust her.

Steve Jacobsen,
Co-Director of La Casa De Maria Retreat
and Conference Center, Santa Barbara

INTRODUCTION

As a therapist who has walked the journey with hundreds of grievers, I reflect upon the reason our sessions are so beneficial to my clients. Primarily, it's about our relationship.

My clients know that I care deeply about their loss and their healing process. They know that they can count on me to be a constant and caring presence for as long as the journey takes. They know I understand the process and can gently guide them on their grief journey, giving them practical tools and wisdom along the way.

How do these deeply personal relationships translate into a book?

I want you to know that I truly care about the sadness and loss that you feel. The purpose of this book is to let you know that every complex feeling you experience is normal in the grief process. If you can grasp this idea, if you can reflect on your journey from a vantage point of "normal," then you can survive grief in the healthiest way possible.

In this book, I will give you an overview of the dangers, the pitfalls, and the highs and lows of your journey ahead. I will provide tools to help survive Courage Road. And if you do the grief work and trust the healing process, I am confident you will find light at the end of the Road.

Let me be your guide.

> "Mary was my facilitator for the Widows' group. In my darkest moments, alone at night, I held on to Mary's promise that I would heal. I trusted her to be my light when I did not believe there was light at the end of the Road. It's still a journey, but I see light and I feel lighter."—Julie.

HOW TO USE THIS BOOK

I want this guide to be easy and readable since grievers often have difficulty concentrating. Therefore, please do not get bogged down or overwhelmed if a concept does not apply to you. Don't fight it; just move along. It may become relevant at another point along the Road. Also, do not get bogged down with semantics. For example, I may use emotions and feelings interchangeably. There is a difference, but not enough of a difference to debate at this stage of your grief process.

Though there are many kinds of loss, such as financial loss, pet loss, loss of friendships or trust, or loss from a house fire, and in their own way, all produce grief, this book specifically focuses on the grief that comes from the loss of a loved one.

The **TRAVELERS' TALES** are a compilation of stories from the hundreds of clients that I have walked Courage Road with in individual and group sessions. Their nuggets of wisdom are invaluable to others on the Road. Many of the feelings, descriptions, and tips overlap in their relevance. You can pick up and read any page at any time and something will apply to you. For the most part, I have not separated specific types of grief, such as sudden and unexpected death, child loss, cancer, or suicide. I acknowledge that the complexities of grief are different for each type of loss. However, many generalities apply, and that is what I emphasize here. I want to reach as many bereaved as possible who must sadly embark on the journey down Courage Road.

Throughout this guide, there are references to "doing your grief work." This means using all the tools in your Backpack as you begin the journey. You will find the tools throughout the guide embedded in the text and clearly marked. In addition, make use of the What's In Your Backpack chapter, starting on page 133. The more you utilize the tools you pick up along the Road, the smoother—not necessarily less painful—your path will be.

PART ONE: THE ROAD BECKONS

 ## THE COMPLEXITY OF GRIEF

Heartbreak, fear, anguish, sorrow, confusion, emptiness, guilt, overwhelmingness are only a few of the ways to describe grief. These emotions hit you to your core. They leave you reeling, perhaps unable to concentrate on work or take care of other relationships. These are just some common emotions that are normal and expected when someone close to you dies. In fact, death may not be the only trigger for these emotions. Often, the diagnosis or threat of death is enough to turn your insides to jelly. From one minute to the next, from one day to the next, these intense emotions will rise and fall, take center stage and retreat, ebb and flow.

The question I am most often asked is how long grief will last. People ask with the hope that I will relieve some of their pain. My usual response is that it will last longer than you or anyone close to you wants it to.

What you can expect, most likely, but certainly depending on numerous factors, is a long road of different emotions. In fact, there are as many different kinds of grief experiences as there are individuals. For example a widow not only loses her spouse but, in many cases, her identity, her financial security, and her best friend. A person who loses a close friend or relative to suicide has another layer of complication often dealing with the Why's and What If's. The loss of a child of any age—well, there are hardly words to describe this kind of loss. The grief journey is a process. If you want to accommodate to your loss with as few scars as possible, you must have the courage to travel down the Road. I call it Courage Road.

Before you can travel Courage Road, you need to understand the process of grieving and what it means to do grief work.

This may appear obvious at first, but those who are in the throes of deep grief understand that the process is much more time consuming, exhausting, and complicated than they might have expected. So many facets and levels of grief will arise that are unique to you and to the relationship that you had with your loved one. Additionally, the events currently shaping your life play a part in how you grieve.

> When my mother died one month before my first child was born, I had little time to grieve. I put my grief on the back burner in order to adjust to the overwhelming responsibilities of a new baby with colic. Several years later when my dad died, I was going through a painful divorce. It was confusing to separate the pain of those two losses. I had no tools to help me through the process. I was unaware that there was any "work" to be done.
>
> If I had understood about grief work after my mom died, (that is, using an array of tools to help accommodate to the loss) then it would have been smoother when my dad passed. I would have been better equipped to handle his loss. This does not mean that I would have missed him less.

More often than not, the process of grieving and healing is the biggest and most difficult challenge you will face in life. It is important to note that grieving and healing are the same process, but healing can happen only when you fully grieve. When you limp along, unguided in your grieving process, you may not fully heal.

Many have spent years crying at the mention of their loved one's name, wondering why they have not healed. It's because they never fully grieved.

The pain can seem unbearable, and continuing your life with any sense of clarity and optimism can seem impossible. But by meeting your grief with courage, an open heart, and with determined patience, you can heal fully. Courage Road is an unchartered, lonely, and rather hazardous path that you can take to heal your broken heart, to resolve your unanswered questions and conflicts, and at the right time, to begin creating your new life.

 FINDING YOUR COURAGE

To travel Courage Road, you must be willing to travel through dark scary forests, explore rugged mountains, cross deep valleys, and brave raging rivers. You will hit potholes and other unexpected roadblocks that will impede your progress. You will have to push through and find your way around them.

This road takes courage because you will face very painful emotions and thoughts, and you will find that they may occur in sudden and unpredictable bursts, just when you feel you are making good progress. Sometimes this can leave you stunned, gasping for breath, your heart racing. Your sleep may suffer, and your food may taste like cardboard. You may feel that you will never be able to get beyond this recurring state of despair and hopelessness.

It takes courage to look at a photograph of your loved one, remembering the sweetest memories. Although these memories will be remembered for some time, the opportunity to make new ones will never occur again. It takes courage to go to work to pay bills when all you want to do is sit and stare at a wall. It takes courage to look at your guilty feelings and decide whether the guilt is justified, and if so, it especially takes courage to allow it to turn into regret and then forgiveness.

You have the choice whether or not to step onto this path. Because the Road is hard, some will decide it is too painful a journey. They may wall off this loss in a part of their mind and heart. They may believe they will deal with it when they are stronger or when it is more convenient. But grief is not convenient. How many times do the tears spill over while you are standing in the checkout line? You only get stronger when you are doing the work. If you deny this process, I can assure you that it will leak out in some other ways, like inappropriate anger or irritability or illness.

Your grieving and healing process will take longer than you want and longer than others want too. Allow yourself the time to grieve in a healthy way. The reward is worth it both psychologically and physically.

Learning how to grieve fully will prove invaluable throughout your life.

 ## THE IMPACT OF LOSS

It is a fact that grief compromises your immune system, even if you are doing grief work. While many people understand that the grief process can continue for a protracted period, few consider the process holistically.

Loss has a profound impact on the whole body and mind. After all, the separation from your loved one is not only emotional, but also physical and permanent. This is especially true for those who have lost a partner, child, or family member who shared a home with them. Grief alters the body and mind by affecting appetite and sleep, and it can make people forgetful, accident prone, and irritable. All of this profoundly impacts the immune system, blood pressure, and other physiological processes. We have all heard about people who die soon after a beloved spouse or about people developing an illness shortly after suffering a loss.

Though it is normal to feel vulnerable, both emotionally and physically, if a person is in poor health before they suffer loss, then they can be especially prone to exacerbating their condition. However, it is not uncommon for previous complaints to go into remission during the initial period of mourning either. This is because loss overshadows all else for a time.

Any grieving person is actually risking their own health, no matter how healthy they were previously.

For example, world-class ocean swimmer Lynne Cox is able to withstand freezing temperatures in Antarctica because of her exceptional health. However, after the deaths of her parents and her beloved dog, she became very ill. She was diagnosed with a condition called broken heart syndrome. It should be noted that Lynne was the primary caregiver for both parents.

Anyone who has been a caregiver understands the depth of stress on one's health. This condition is completely reversible, but it illustrates how vital it is for people to take care of themselves every day. You may have little motivation to do so, but know that it will pay big dividends if you do.

Particular attention should be paid to getting adequate sleep, to relaxation, and to good nutrition—especially eating green vegetables every day and drinking plenty of water to replace the tears shed. Breathing often becomes shallow. Remember to breathe, taking deeper, longer breaths. Do not overindulge in anything, whether it be chocolate, alcohol, or something else. Balance and moderation are key.

THE TRANSFORMATION OF GRIEF

Grief is a profoundly transformative process that cannot be rushed. It is wise to take a lesson from nature. It takes a caterpillar time to spin a cocoon and a period of overwhelming change to become a butterfly. What would be the result if the cocoon were forced open before the process was completed? Use this metaphor of the cocoon, or imagine a sturdy tent as a place to go when you feel vulnerable, misunderstood, or if you need peace and quiet. Trust your gut to know when you need to go into your cocoon or tent. Go in and out of your cocoon or tent during the whole grief journey. It is your safe space to be authentic and comfortable with your feelings for as long as you need to. Do not let anyone coax you out sooner than you are ready.

If you are brave enough to take Courage Road, which means facing the pain and doing grief work, then you may eventually come to a place of healing, wisdom, and insight that you may not have thought possible.

But you will only arrive by taking one step at a time. Like most natural process-es, there is a rhythmic ebb and flow to this process. It is not a straight linear line from point to point. You need to recognize this and allow yourself to feel the impact of your loss, then allow yourself to retreat into your safe cocoon for a rest. Allowing rest is a part of grief work and is essential for healing.

PART TWO: YOUR BACKPACK

- Loops of Recovery
- Feelings Pass, Feelings Change
- The Wave Metaphor
- Trust the Healing Process

As you walk Courage Road, you will need to take along a Backpack filled with supplies to make your journey smoother. In this section, I will introduce essential concepts and tools. Some of these tools you may have to learn and some are common sense that one forgets when in the throes of grief. Therefore, review what is in your Backpack frequently. Part Five explains the tools more thoroughly. Take a look at that now.

LOOPS OF RECOVERY

The Loops of Recovery (see appendix) is the first concept I teach my clients. They tell me that it is the most valuable piece of information that I give them.

Because grief is so painful, we want to heal quickly. We want to reach the end of the grief journey as smoothly as possible—a freeway to the light at the end of the Road with no bumps, no potholes, no stormy conditions. But alas, usually every kind of road and weather condition pops up on Courage Road. This is the reality of grief. How you deal with it will determine how smooth the road becomes.

What is important to remember is that when you hit a barrier, detour, or adverse road condition, it should not throw you back to the very beginning of the journey. It may feel that way, but consider that you have already picked up skills to add to your Backpack to carry you further along the Road. Each time you practice self-care or respond to an insensitive comment with polite assertiveness, then you gain necessary strength to step forward along the path. When you are slammed with

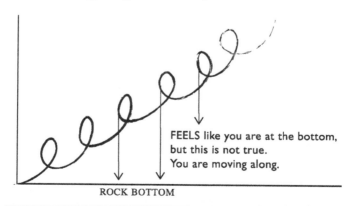

FEELS like you are at the bottom, but this is not true. You are moving along.

ROCK BOTTOM

LOOPS OF RECOVERY

despair or regret, you will have some tools to gently move through those huge emotions. Remember that you are not going back to the very bottom, even though *it may feel that way.*

 ## FEELINGS PASS AND FEELINGS CHANGE

Feelings are just feelings. They are neither right nor wrong. They pass, they change, and they can lie.

Your strong feelings may feel true and valid in the moment, but give yourself a bit of time and perspective, then the feelings will pass. They may come back again soon after or later on, but feelings do pass. For example, "This is too much to bear. I can never recover from this tragic loss. I have made no progress whatsoever," may feel true at this moment in time, but this is a prime example of Stinkin' Thinkin' or Distorted Thinking. (See Detour of Stinkin' Thinkin' and Appendix.) But these strong feelings will change and pass and shift and morph.

This is important to remember when you are on a downward loop and it feels that you have made no progress. But trust that you are making progress.

How do feelings lie? (See Page 59 under the terrain of Cliff.)

 # THE WAVE METAPHOR

It helps to see grief as a powerful force of nature, like waves that hit you again and again. Just like learning to swim in the ocean, you learn to handle the first wave so the next wave does not drown you. The waves will keep coming until the storm passes. Sometimes the waves will feel more like a tsunami. You must learn to dive through the wave, and it will pass as it always does.

Let me explain using this analogy: if you swim in the ocean, you quickly learn that when a big wave approaches, you cannot run for shore or puff out your chest and brace against it. The wave is a force of nature that you have to learn to work with, no matter how scary. It feels as though it may crush you when you watch it approach. But if you dive through the wave, it passes. Our instinct is to run, but we cannot outrun a force of nature. So, learn to accept the waves of grief.

Take advantage of the lulls between them, take a deep breath, but be ready for the next wave.

I want to clarify this concept. I am not suggesting that you put your head down, hold your breath, and get on with things until it ends. It is, in fact, the opposite. When these powerful feelings surface, however painful at the time, in the long run it is more helpful to embrace rather than reject them. Accept them willingly rather than push them away. These feelings are not problems to "get over" as quickly as possible. Because these feelings are normal, allow them to run their natural course. When you do this, you will come out the other side, perhaps not faster, but certainly less scarred. The trick is to allow yourself to feel your feelings without becoming consumed by them. Paying attention to the Travelers' Tips will help you navigate this difficult journey.

Sometimes the waves come when it is not convenient and you may need to postpone diving in. Sometimes there is good reason to delay.

> For example, if you are doing a presentation at work and suddenly catch a whiff of the fragrance that your wife wore. This is a wave that is inappropriate to dive through at that specific moment. You may need to take a moment to recover by shuffling papers, sipping water, taking a deep breath, and then resuming the presentation. You can let the tears fall when you get to your car. Your car can be a safe cocoon for the moment.

> Example Two: You are going down an aisle at the market and see the box of gingerbread cookies that your mom always had on hand. Although the grief

wave is hitting you strongly, this is not the time for a meltdown. This is the time to employ some of the tools you are learning about. Take a deep breath, tell yourself you can make it through, and focus on the next item on your list. Then when you arrive home, allow the tears to flow.

In both these examples, you must dive into these strong feelings only when you are able. This means that you shouldn't push them away forever. You sit with them, identify them, and allow them to surface, however painful they may be.

Think about doing something physically difficult— holding a Yoga pose, carrying a heavy box up from the basement, taking off a tight lug nut. You endure the difficult action until it is completed. It is the same with holding a strong emotion until it passes. You can talk to yourself and coach yourself. "You can do it. This will pass. Hang in there." You may want to grab a pen and write about the feelings that are arising. Courage Road requires deep, loving reflection and time to digest.

In response to telling one of my clients that she needs to sit with her strong feelings instead of running away from them she said, "That's like telling me to sit on this hot stove, stay there, and eventually it will cool down!" Yes. I realize it seems like that, and I know it sounds like an impossible task, but I promise you that it is a necessary task. Remember, the grief wave passes. The stove does cool down. There will be times that you may need to turn down the heat to low to give yourself a temporary detour from the intensity of the Road. Sometimes when the waves are too overpowering, it is okay to give yourself a break by distracting yourself. Find your necessary balance.

 TRUST THE HEALING PROCESS

If you look at the Loops of Recovery, you can see the trajectory of healing. A bereaved person has moments, hours, or days that he may feel okay. That is the up-swing in the loop on the diagram.

Then, usually without warning, that person is assaulted by a grief wave. The grief wave can be so intense that their knees will buckle, or perhaps they're hit with incomprehensible disbelief or a longing so profound that even survival feels distant. This is the downward part of the loop.

But if you trust the healing process, the process that has been happening since the beginning of time, then you will notice that if you dive through the wave and not stuff it or medicate it, then the wave will pass and eventually the loop will go upward again.

As more upward loops are experienced, it is possible to look back and see how far you have come. When a grief wave hits, whether through strong feelings or life circumstances, it may not feel that you have made progress. It may feel that you are at the very bottom, but this is not true. You are gaining skill, strength, time, and perspective which furthers you along Courage Road.

🄷 TRAVELER'S TIP

I strongly recommend that you keep a grief journal. It will help you explore your strong feelings. Then later, you can look back at what you write, and it will give you perspective on your journey. Try to write as often as possible, even if it is just a few sentences. Write during the down loops as well as during the up loops. When the up loops occur, write down what you are feeling and what insights you may be experiencing.

Note any feelings that are more positive than negative. Look for something for which you can be grateful. Be aware of any beauty that you see—a sunset or a hummingbird, perhaps. Savor this up loop experience a little longer and really let it sink in. If you can focus on this kind of exercise, then you are rewiring your brain toward the positive, helping you to build your internal resources, which aid along the Road. Brain studies have confirmed that we can change the way we think, which

---

then impacts the way we feel. This means that when you are on a down loop, you can look at your grief journal to remind you that you are not at rock bottom and that, indeed, you have made progress.

PART THREE: DETOURS OFF COURAGE ROAD

- Delay or Procrastination
- Denial
- Overachiever Griever
- Dishonoring the Memory
- Numbsville
- Bad Advice
- Stinkin' Thinkin'
- Busyness
- Complication

In this section, I will describe detours that grievers start to wander down. Some of these detours are normal, some are destructive, some are due to personality types or the circumstances that currently affect your life. Whatever the reason, if you pay attention to signs that you are on a detour, you can eventually make your way back to Courage Road.

DETOUR OF DELAY OR PROCRASTINATION

There are times when delaying grief work is necessary. When life circumstances overtake grief and you have no choice but to deal with those circumstances first, then you must do what you must. Here are some examples: You are an accountant in the middle of tax season. Too many people are counting on you, including your family to put food on the table. When tax season ends, do your grief work. Or maybe you have just received a life-threatening diagnosis. Take care of yourself first. Then do your grief work.

There are other times that delaying is unnecessary. Procrastination and avoidance, although common, can work against progress in your healing. Although being in the world may feel surreal, it is, in fact, reality. You may not want to open mail and pay bills, but if you don't, then it will cause more pain in the future.

> It is important to allow yourself to oscillate between being in reality—that is, paying your bills, eating a healthy meal, taking care of your kids, feeding the pet, etc.—and retreating to your safe cocoon or sturdy tent, perhaps to explore your emotions and thoughts about this loss.

Both are necessary to make progress on your journey. Perhaps you do not feel strong enough to face the pain. However, you will only get stronger by doing the grief work and utilizing the tools in your Backpack. Think about carrying a heavy boulder along with you on the Road. As you continue to carry it, your muscles get stronger.

Delaying or procrastinating is more of a conscious decision whereas the next path, Denial, is out of your control. Sometimes these two paths feel similar.

DETOUR OF DENIAL

Denial can serve a constructive purpose. It is one way you are unconsciously taking care of yourself. It allows your body and mind to catch up, so to speak. Some choose to take the grief journey one step at a time, finding it too overwhelming or frightening to look down the long Road ahead. However, such an approach may leave them unprepared for the pitfalls that lie in wait. Others want to know exactly what to expect, even if it is painful to hear.

One of my former clients wisely said, "Grief is too big to swallow whole. You have to take it in bite-sized pieces." Fortunately, our body's innate intelligence helps us to do this naturally. This is why some grievers might do okay for the first few months. This is the time when grievers may hear silly comments like, "You're doing so well. You are so strong." When I tell people that the pain might become worse in a few months, they look at me in disbelief and anger. "How could I possibly feel worse?" But the truth is that most people automatically become numb to a certain extent immediately following death. You cannot realize this until you look back. When the numbness wears off, then you begin to feel the permanence and the complexity of loss.

Even the words "died" or "death" feel too harsh, too permanent. That is why so many people prefer euphemisms such as "loss" and "passed on." I, too, use some of those softer words in this book for this very reason.

Some grievers prefer to stay in denial forever. They are not doing their grief work. That is avoidance. It will eventually catch up to them in some form or another.

DETOUR OF THE OVERACHIEVER GRIEVER

Many of my clients who tend to be primarily either of the Type As—Perfectionists or List Makers—try to convince themselves that they can shortcut the process. They may arrive at our session with notebook in hand asking for the steps to get out of their pain. They want to be an A student in how to grieve. Or perhaps they are used to living life with a list of goals to check off as they accomplish them; they want to put a check mark on "Completed Grief Process. Whew!"

There is no shortcut. It takes the time it takes.

I honor the work that Elizabeth Kubler-Ross did to bring light to the death and dying process. However, she never meant for those stages of grief to be interpreted as we have interpreted them. The stages are meant for those who are dying, not for grievers. There are phases that many grievers go through that are similar, but not everyone must go through these phases. And they are certainly not in any linear order.

DETOUR LEADING TO NUMBSVILLE

It is understandable to want to numb your painful feelings. Let's face it, our culture as a whole does not do well with pain—neither emotional nor physical. But, I promise you that this kind of pain cannot be covered up without consequences further down the Road. There are numerous ways to numb yourself. Some include using alcohol, drugs, the Internet, video games, shopping, exercise, and food—anything you overindulge in to keep from feeling the feelings.

Grieving is painful. Doing the grief work is painful. But if you do the hard work, which means diving into the pain with the proper support and tools, then you can come out the other side in the healthiest way possible. Do you really want to delay what will catch up to you in some form down the Road? Grief is a natural process of life. It is also bigger than you are. You cannot control it as surely as you cannot control a force of nature.

DETOUR OF BAD ADVICE

Listening to bad advice may throw you off the healthy path. "Buck up," or "No more tears," or "Get on with life," or "Get over it," or "Your loved one would want you to be strong now," are all ridiculous pieces of advice. Your grief must be expressed in a healthy way to help you work through to a healing and hopeful place.

Tears are a natural release valve. There are many different ways to express grief, which will be addressed later. The most powerful healing comes when a griever can safely express to another person the many different facets and complexities of what they are experiencing. To be helpful, that listener should be able to listen without judgment or without trying to fix the other person. These emotions must be expressed to and witnessed by a person who sincerely and lovingly cares.

This is why going to a good support group is important. Not only are you with people who understand, but they also see your pain, acknowledge it, and validate it. As an infant, a parent mirrors back love by imitating the baby's coo. Children become emotionally healthy when the parent is saying "Good job!" What child wants to dive off the diving board if no one is watching and giving praise? When a child skins his knee, a good parent is there to comfort them. Even posts on Facebook expect a "like," which represents that someone has seen what is important to the poster.

So when a griever is met with dismissive comments or their pain is not acknowledged in a way that comforts, then healing may be stalled. Seek appropriate validation and understanding of the difficult Road you are on. Find a good grief counselor or support group (even online is better than nothing).When we love on a scale of one, then we grieve on a scale of one. When we love at a five, we grieve at a five, and when we love at a ten, we grieve at a ten. Grief is part of the human experience, especially when we love.

St. Augustine wrote, "The tears... streamed down, and I let them flow as freely as they would, making of them a pillow for my heart. On them it rested."

DETOUR OF STINKIN' THINKIN'

All of us have forms of stinkin', or distorted, thinking. When we are feeling especially emotional and vulnerable, like when we are grieving, then the distortions are even more pronounced. You may feel that your thoughts are true at the time, however, under deep emotional distress, one does not think clearly. Facts and reality are often misrepresented or blurry. Similar to seeing yourself in a carnival mirror, your body is distorted into a squat rotund self or an elongated person. You see a representation of yourself that is not completely accurate.

Thoughts about self-blame, guilt, or having no purpose

are examples of distorted thinking and are often part of the normal process of grief. We look for answers, understanding, reasons, and closure. This is the way our brain works. It is normal to do this for a period of time. However, at some point down the Road, it will be wise to challenge your stinkin' thinkin'.

Saying that nothing matters or that you no longer care about anything are sentiments that I have heard many times. However, from my experience, you will care about something eventually. Something or someone will matter to you one day. In fact, you may start to matter to you.

Self-blame is another detour that beckons frequently. Initially, you may drive yourself crazy with thoughts like, "I should have done something different," or "I failed." This process is normal and difficult to avoid. But you must begin to entertain the possibility that your thoughts are distorted. Plant those seeds. Then work with a therapist or book that will teach you to challenge these distortions and over time allow you to release them.

TIP BOX

Do not let distorted thinking throw you too far off Courage Road. Learn to challenge these thoughts. See Appendix—Stinkin' Thinkin'.

DETOUR OF BUSYNESS

Staying busy can help quell the pain, but it will not extinguish it. You cannot outrun it. You eventually have to slow down and come face to face with it. Find the right balance between action and contemplation. Being with your thoughts can be exhausting or scary, but necessary.

Later, I will identify many of the different types of feelings associated with grief. It is important to "sit with" and experience these different feelings. With practice, it will become easier. In time, you will adapt and accommodate to your loss.

DETOUR OF COMPLICATION

Grief is much more complicated than we often expect. The many different facets and layers of grief that arise over time are exhausting and overwhelming. Some people may not know where to begin to sort it all out, so they give up before starting any kind of grief work.

Everyone's grief journey is different for many different reasons. Sometimes it depends on the relationship you had with the deceased. It may have been a close and loving relationship. Or perhaps it was contentious and conflicted, and you are left with unfinished business. The idea that families will unite after the loss of a loved one often does not correspond to reality. Frequently, a family unit can explode with greed and misunderstandings, and past grudges will come to the forefront. Sometimes family members can be supportive of one another. But at other times, individuals are too raw within their own grief to be able to tend to the needs of others.

Numerous other issues may arise after someone dies which makes life complicated. These issues may be related to your grief or they may be completely unrelated life issues. Problems will sometimes resolve themselves without you having to struggle over them. On numerous occasions, my clients will have a particular issue dominate our session that appears unsolvable. When I ask about the issue during our next session, my clients often look at me puzzled and say something like, "Oh that! No, that got resolved. Now it's something else." I am often amazed at how problems resolve themselves when grief work is being done simultaneously.

Another complication happens when you experience more than one death within a close period of time. In such circumstances, it can be difficult for the bereaved to know who to grieve for first. It becomes confusing. The good news is that when you decide to take it one layer, one facet, one problem at a time, your grief work becomes doable.

It is easy to take detours. They beckon you, and sometimes they serve a purpose for a while—like denial, which protects you and softens the blow from reality for a period of time. But recognizing that you are on a detour is necessary if you are to get back on the Road. Awareness, even in the midst of your shock and fog, is key on Courage Road.

TRAVELER'S TALE

"After my mom died, my friends were very consoling for a few months. But then they started asking, 'Do you feel better?' like I had the flu or something. They think that just because my mom was older and lived a long life that I shouldn't be grieving. But I believe I have every right to grieve. I have to be patient with my friends. They have good intentions, even though they have no clue."

PART FOUR: RECOGNIZING AND NAVIGATING ROAD CONDITIONS— *THE TERRAIN*

- Torrential Rain—*Sorrow*
- Dark Forest—*Lost*
- Paralysis Point—*Helplessness*
- Mud Hole—*Detachment*
- Cliff—*Despair*
- Cactus Patch—*Anxiety*
- Hurricane—*Crazy Feelings*
- Underbrush—*Worry or Fear*
- Hermit's Cave—*Isolation*
- Thunder and Lightning—*Dread*
- Quicksand—*Overwhelmingness*
- Haunted Woods—*Obsession*

- Freezing Temperatures— *Numbness*
- Volcano— *Bottling It Up*
- Bridge to Nowhere— *Guilt*
- Rickety Bridge— *Incompetence or Self-Doubt*
- Clinging to an Unattached Rope— *Staying Attached to Grief*
- Tornado— *Control*
- Earthquake— *Shock and Trauma*
- Swampland— *Shame*
- Desert— *Loneliness*
- Forest Fire— *Anger*
- Rugged Mountain— *Blame*
- Minefield— *Family Drama*
- Sour Berries— *Bitterness*
- Broken Compass— *Confusion*
- Field of Flowers— *Relief*

Grief has many facets, just like a prism. Anger, guilt, sorrow, and fear, for example, may pop up at any time and without warning. Throughout the period of bereavement and healing, the prism of grief will keep turning to reveal its different facets. You will struggle with one facet for a while, and you may feel that you are fully stuck.

But here is what you can count on—what you are struggling with will change. It always does. Where you are in the process today will not be where you will be in a week, in a month, or even in a year. Change may not always feel better or worse. It will just feel different.

In this section, I will identify the common feelings and thoughts that surface repeatedly during the grieving process. Look for these commonalities in italics at the beginning of each new terrain. I will also add common life circumstances that may impede your progress on Courage Road. As you identify the circumstances that resonate with you, you will see that other travelers have had a similar journey and they survived. Even though grief can be a lonely journey, the more you can connect and recognize your experience in others, the lighter your load will be.

I will define common facets of grief one by one, in no

particular order. In keeping with the Road metaphor, these facets represent a territory on the grief map. Keep in mind that you do not have to experience all of these facets. Some may surface at a later time, often when you least expect it. However, when you do experience one of these strong thoughts or feelings or one of these grief waves, you must dive through it.

Remember, you must embrace it, look at it from all sides, chew on it, digest it, write about it, call a friend or counselor who will allow you to lean in and not minimize or try to wipe away what you are going through. Again, as you dive through each wave, you are building your skills and allowing the healing to take place. Trust the healing process. These waves will pass.

The road appears dark and scary, but after each terrain, I will give you tools to put in your Backpack. It is important to implement these tools and **TRAVELERS' TIPS**. Just reading about them will not ease your journey. You must also take some action. Some tools are gentle, like remembering to take a breath. Some require that you grab a pen and do some writing. The tools will seem repetitive, but this is necessary and purposeful. You may find it helpful to review this section in the months ahead as the landscape on your Road changes.

So hop in your metaphorical Jeep or grab your walking stick and hiking boots, put on your Backpack packed with your essential tools (See Part Five for complete list), and let's begin this journey together.

NATURE
Patience Loops HYDRATE
Replace stinkin' thinkin'
COCOON Move
TRUST THE HEALING PROCESS
Breath Self-Care
Moderation Courage
DIVE THROUGH THE WAVES
EAT GOOD FOOD Journal
Gratitude SLEEP
GREEN HAIR TRICK Teflon mind
Don't SHOULD on yourself Support

TORRENTIAL RAIN
SORROW

The word sadness does not begin to describe the depth of sorrow that I feel. My world is colorless, flat, empty. My heart is broken and aches.

I had always heard that the Eskimos have one hundred or so different words for snow (now I hear this is false), so our language should have more words to describe how grief feels. "Heartbroken" and "devastated" are words that try to express the enormity of your sorrow, but whatever you call it, it is an all-pervasive, painful feeling that floods your whole world for a time like a torrential rain.

Sorrow covers the whole map of grief. It is what makes a griever unable to see light at the end of the Road. Sorrow is dark and gloomy. So with courage and support, dive into the sorrow. Your loved one deserves a period of mourning. The griever's sadness is a

GRIEF

It touches everything.
It is in
My scrambled eggs,
Buying a quart of milk instead of a gallon,
Loading and unloading the dishwasher,
Taking out the trash,
Feeding the cat who constantly looks for him.
It is under my pillow,
In his coffee pot,
In my clothes that no longer fit,
In the face that looks back at me in the mirror.

I am a puddle of miserable self,
I show up with an ache of grief that is just beneath the surface
of my skin,
Ready to ooze out my eyes and scream from my closed mouth.
Grief is on his side of the bed that is filled with his pillow to
hug and books on grief and
Prayers to try to feel him solid in my shattered heart.

I have flashes of peace and the profound feeling of his love
But
Grief has teeth and scales and claws and fiery breath just
waiting to be unleashed.
Grief steals my brain,
Grief make me stupid,
Lures me into feeling safe then it strikes with vengeance.

I know I must learn to live with this beast.

By Susan Cochran, used with permission

DARK FOREST
LOST

I feel lost. Everything that felt familiar now feels unfamiliar. It feels surreal. My world has changed; it's upside down. There are no markers.

I feel like a ship without a rudder looking for a safe port. Where do I fit in now? What is my role now?

It is normal to feel disoriented in time and space initially after loss. It feels as if everyone is moving on, but you are not ready to move on. Although it is intense and you want to shed the pain, your brain has not yet caught up with your heart. You are not able to grasp the loss, and you just want everyone to wait until you have your bearings again. As time passes, you may begin to feel solid ground again, until the next time a grief wave appears and you feel swept off your feet. Remember that this is how it works. Grief is an ebb and flow.

Rumi, the wise thirteenth-century Persian poet, said it best:

> This being human is a guest house.
> Every morning a new arrival.
> A joy, a depression, a meanness,
> some momentary awareness comes
> as an unexpected visitor.
>
> Welcome and entertain them all!
> Even if they're a crowd of sorrows,
> who violently sweep your house
> empty of its furniture,
> still treat each guest honorably.
> He may be clearing you out
> for some new delight.
>
> The dark thought, the shame, the malice,
> meet them at the door laughing,
> and invite them in.
>
> Be grateful for whoever comes,
> because each has been sent
> as a guide from beyond.

PARALYSIS POINT
HELPLESSNESS

I cannot cope with the smallest things in my life. I need help with everything, and I'm too embarrassed to ask. I feel like a baby, and I want to be a baby and have someone just take care of me. Could someone just take out the garbage for me because even that seems too much to handle. Sometimes I do not know what I need to do or what I have already done! My mind is mush.

Be gentle with your thoughts about yourself.

After all, you are in unchartered territory, and Paralysis Point has you stuck at this point along Courage Road until you do something about it. You have suffered a blow to your body and psyche. The desire to be comforted and taken care of is a natural consequence of this blow. If you have a supportive group of people or even one friend offering to take care of some things for you, then receive this help and be thankful.

TRAVELER'S TIP

Be aware of any insights or strengths that occur during an up loop. These will occur naturally, and most grievers are unaware that these little shifts even take place. Try to become more aware. Enjoy the upward loops. But remember that healing is not a straight line up. Also, be mindful that a down loop awaits you. Being mindful means that you will not feel so assaulted or upended when a down loop occurs.

MUD HOLE
DETACHMENT

Everything seems unreal, as if this is happening to someone else. The world feels surreal. I pass through each hour, each day mechanically, robotically, sometimes in slow motion, as if moving through mud. I feel heavy.

Time is distorted. It feels as though the loss has happened months ago, and at the same time it feels like it just happened yesterday. Everything is unfathomable. The days feel unbearably long. How will I make it through the next season? I feel that my loved one should walk through the door at any moment. My head, heart, and body do not feel connected.

This sense of non-reality happens to everyone. Isn't it amazing that life goes on, that people still go to the grocery store or that grievers even get out of bed in the morning? The passage of time is a strange phenomenon. But it is a part of the healing process that will layer of complexity when someone is dealing with the aftermath of suicide.

Remember the important tool that you put in your Backpack—Feelings pass, feelings change, and feelings can lie.

How do feelings lie? With grief, you start to believe the negative things that you tell yourself. I will never get over this. My life has no purpose. This pain is too great. I will not be able to survive it. These thoughts and feelings feel true. But let me tell you the reality: many of the hundreds of grievers who I have accompanied on their journey felt utterly hopeless, and they were eventually able to heal.

They realized that their feelings were lying or that their feelings changed or that their situation changed. Something shifted that took them out of despair and into bearable and down the Road into hope. As I have mentioned previously, healing is uniquely defined for every individual.

Those who are in despair and anguish must give it time, because with time and support, your feelings will shift. Do not buy into thinking that your situation is unique. You are not the only person who has suffered this kind of despair. Death happens under tragic circumstances, leaving wreckage in its wake.

Trust the timeless truth: people heal and allow love in their hearts. You do not have to think too far in the future at this moment. Stay in the present until this despair passes.

Remember that feelings feel true at the time but feelings pass, feelings change, and feelings can lie.

Sometimes it feels like it is too much to think "one day at a time." Sometimes you can only manage one minute at a time. But if you string these minutes together, they become hours, days, and weeks. Then you begin to make it through. It may seem impossible, but it is possible. Eventually, you will find yourself backing further and further away from the cliff.

🧰 🔭 TRAVELER'S TIP

Try to expand your heart even in the midst of your pain. Go to a vista point either physically or metaphorically and remember that out there in the big world there is suffering and sadness, and there is also beauty and compassion. If possible, deepen your love for family, friends, community, country, humankind, animal kind. Find something to be grateful for.

visualization, hypnotherapy, breathing and relaxation techniques, acupuncture, cranial-sacral therapy, meditation, and prayer to help with your anxiety.

In my experience, grievers without pre-existing anxiety issues may find that these symptoms are transitory, as with other symptoms of grief. Like the facets that appear, then recede, then reappear, anxiety may be like that for you. It will help if you use those aforementioned alternative practices. Find out which work for you and commit to practicing with those tools. These kinds of tools only work with conscious and diligent practice. And with practice, many people find relief.

Do not catch yourself on the thorns of anxiety. The cactus patch is a profound image of a place you do not want to dwell. Get relief now to work through this patch so you can return to Courage Road.

TRAVELER'S TIP
You must challenge the validity of your anxious thoughts. Also, getting some exercise, even if it is only taking a walk around the block, will be of benefit. Something is better than nothing at all. Please see Appendix on Stinkin' Thinkin'. If, on the other hand, you have a pre-existing diagnosis and/or you are not managing your symptoms with alternative therapies, please consult your doctor.

HURRICANE
CRAZY FEELINGS

I feel like I'm going crazy, and I'm utterly exhausted. I can't remember the simplest thing from one moment to the next. I lose my car keys daily. This behavior is so uncharacteristic for me. I feel afraid that I'm losing my mind.

Many people tell me that they fear they are actually going crazy. Why is that? I believe it is because there are so many intense and unfamiliar feelings being experienced all at once that affect everything you do. If these emotions were experienced neatly and slowly, one at a time, maybe you could handle them.

But instead, they hit like a hurricane, and the winds are relentless. Feelings get mixed up with thoughts, memories, and fears that all contribute to the craziness. When these get added on top of all the responsibili-

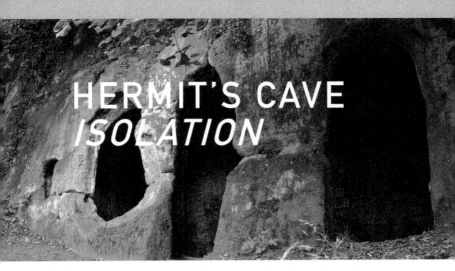

HERMIT'S CAVE
ISOLATION

I feel like I need to stay away from people altogether since no one understands the depth of my sorrow or knows how to help. I don't want to keep pretending I'm okay, so I just don't answer the phone. People irritate me and impose what they think is best for me. Even when people are nice enough to include me in their plans, I can't be sure that I will have the energy, so I just end up avoiding them. I see people avoiding me too.

If you believe that no one understands your loss and therefore no one can comfort you, then you are practicing what is coined "Terminal Uniqueness." In the end, you may end up completely alone, pushing all your friends away. It may be true that you do not want much social stimulation. You probably feel vulnerable and sensitive. Grief and loss are uncomfortable subjects, and many friends simply do not know how to support you in your loss, and you may stop calling each other.

a good tool because these thoughts bounce around in your head. Unconsciously, you are constantly searching for a solution. Writing down the worry thoughts allows your brain to take a rest, knowing that you can look at the list and resume worrying or finding a solution whenever you want. Do this at night, especially.

Getting proper sleep is essential to the healing process. Let your brain take a rest. If you awake in the middle of the night with worry or terror, then grab your note-pad and do some writing. Writing is an important tool for healing. Then turn off your light and rest assured that you will look at the notes in the morning. With this method, you can stay out of the underbrush and on the clear path. The problem and the solution will wait for you.

🔒 TRAVELER'S TIP

Writing down worry thoughts instead of obsessively thinking about them interrupts the brain pattern. If the thoughts are more obsessive, EMDR (see Part Five: What's In Your Backpack) can be a life-saver. In addition, look at the section on Cognitive tools. Try not to "Future-Trip." I know this is easier said than done, but we cannot control or predict the future. Try to be present in the moment or in the day. Plan something that you can look forward to in the near future.

THUNDER AND LIGHTENING
DREAD

I'm waiting for the other shoe to drop. If someone else I love dies, I don't think I could handle it. New battles emerge, and I keep getting blindsided. I don't feel protected. My beloved died, and I dread going to bed at night. I'm afraid of an empty bed. I'm afraid of recurring nightmares. I dread even going to the market for fear of running into someone I know.

When your current world is colored with all these grief symptoms, then dread and fear are common. When you begin to heal and add more activities and people into your life again, then the dread dissipates.

For me, when the number of grieving clients increased and their tragedies consumed my day, I had difficulty keeping my work and my personal life separated. I feared that something bad was going to happen to one of my loved ones. I could not shake that feeling. How-

*There is too much to deal with. Things feel beyond my
ability to cope. Even the smallest things feel like too much
to do. I want to run away. I want to be rescued. I want my
life back the way it was. It feels like there is no relief; I have
no more room in my pain bucket. I feel like I'm drowning.*

The best way to deal with being overwhelmed is to
take care of yourself. This sounds too simple, but just
consider the consequences if you do not take care of
yourself. Your system will not be able to do the healing,
and you will not be able to function at a higher level
in order to make the decisions that you need to make.
So, this means getting adequate sleep, feeding yourself
properly (comfort food may be necessary but not to
excess), and staying hydrated to offset the loss of those
tears you have shed.

All of this is essential for your brain to work properly.
If your brain does not work properly, then you cannot

covers over their head. Not having the "appropriate look of sadness" can be confusing for others, leading to comments of how strong one is. It usually isn't strength, but numbness.

At this point, some grievers may not be able to access their tears, and they may find that bizarre. It may be your body protecting you until you are ready to bear the pain. In another scenario, perhaps you have been flooded with tears and preoccupied with obsessive thoughts. Now you feel numb. Your body may just be giving you a rest. Give it time, and your tears may arrive when you least expect.

On the other hand, staying numb for too long is not healthy either. It is important to get into balance. Find a safe place (your cocoon or sturdy tent) or person who

allows you the space and time to express your grief without parameters or judgment. By committing to this important tool, you will find the freeze will begin to thaw and the warmth in your body begin to return. Take a moment to imagine how good that might feel.

Expressive art (artwork or music therapy) is often effective in helping shift your emotions and allow the grief to naturally flow out. Do not be afraid of intense or powerful feelings of grief. In whatever form they arrive, they are, in fact, honoring both your loved one and the strength of your love for the one who died. Do they not deserve this period of mourning? You can bear it. Suppressing these feelings and thoughts may create illness in the long run. Release allows for the love in your heart to return.

> ### TRAVELER'S TIP
> Numbness may be a way that your body is protecting you. Give it time. But there are also ways to work on this to allow the feelings to come through.

feel the sunshine upon you. But then you hit a rock. It's called Guilt Rock. You have the choice to grab on, just touch it, or look at it and let it pass.

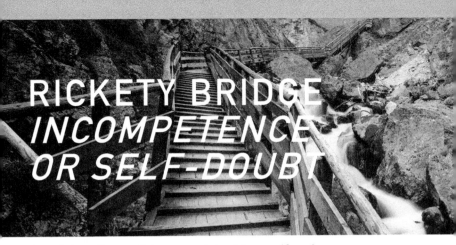

RICKETY BRIDGE *INCOMPETENCE OR SELF-DOUBT*

I can't handle anything now. I doubt myself and my responsibilities. I'm no longer confident, and I can't trust myself to make decisions or follow through on plans. I can't commit to anything. No one understands this, least of all me. I should be a lot further along in my grief journey.

Many grievers have difficulty making and keeping plans because they cannot count on feeling up to it when the time comes. Since grieving is exhausting, many will use up all their energy in the morning then become unable to follow through with a scheduled plan for later. They will feel pressured to follow through, not wanting to appear irresponsible. The best way to handle this is to make as few plans as possible and express in advance the right to withdraw or leave early. Always have a Plan B.

For example, if you go to an event or party or gathering, make sure to drive yourself. That way you can leave

TRAVELER'S TIP

You will acclimate to your loss whether you want to or not. Just don't be pressured to heal too quickly. Remember the metaphor of the butterfly who dies if forced out of the cocoon before it is ready. But also remember to try to balance your life. Moving along in your grief suggests forward movement.

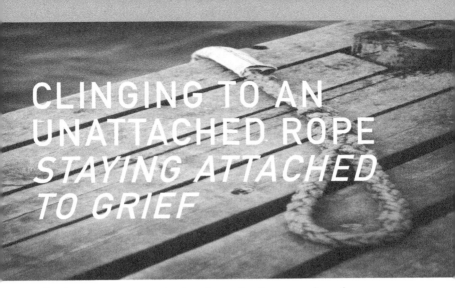

CLINGING TO AN UNATTACHED ROPE
STAYING ATTACHED TO GRIEF

I don't want to stop grieving. I need to keep my loved one in my heart and in my life. Moving on would feel like a betrayal to our love. In some respects, I feel even closer to my loved one now. I'm afraid I will forget.

It is not uncommon for people to feel that they do not want to heal. Some may feel that they do not deserve to heal or that healing means that they will be further disconnected from their loved one. Some people say that as painful as their grief is, it is also a way that they feel close to their loved one. They do not want to lose that closeness.

But slowly, healing occurs whether you like it or not. I don't like the terms "moving on" and "getting over it." I prefer the term "moving along." That means that you can go slowly in your healing process, but there is some

But sometimes because of loss, a person's beliefs are shattered. It may take time to restructure your beliefs or to return to what gave you strength previously.

The fear that results when your assumption of safety is gone can be tremendous and overwhelming. Trust that with time, the tornado will pass, and you will find your way to a new equilibrium. The lesson that may come out of shattered assumptions is that life can change on a dime. Therefore, you must not take life and loved ones for granted.

TRAVELER'S TALE

"My dad was on hospice care in his home and his wish was to die there. But when he began to choke, my brother panicked and called the ambulance. At the hospital, Dad was diagnosed with pneumonia, so he told them to stop food and water and to put him on morphine to die. They followed his wishes, but I still wanted Dad to be able to die at home. The hospital staff said he was too weak to make the trip, and besides, they said he would die any moment. But that didn't happen and after several days, the hospital discharged him because they needed the bed or something. As the ambulance pulled into his driveway, Dad went to be with Mom. I felt so guilty for not being able to control all the factors. It didn't go the way I wanted it to go, but maybe, in the end, it went the way he wanted it."

ALLOW

There is no controlling life.
Try corralling a lightning bolt,
containing a tornado. Dam a
stream and it will create a new
channel. Resist, and the tide
will sweep you off your feet.
Allow, and grace will carry
you to higher ground. The only
safety lies in letting it all in—
the wild and the weak; fear,
fantasies, failures and success.
When loss rips off the doors of
the heart, or sadness veils your
vision with despair, practice
becomes simply bearing the truth.
In the choice to let go of your
known way of being, the whole
world is revealed to your new eyes.

By Danna Faulds, used with permission

of your mind, emotions, and sensibilities. This may even occur when the death is expected and someone witnessed it. "He was breathing and then he wasn't. It was shocking!" Over time you will come out of the shock.

You can expect that after about three months (or longer for certain kinds of losses such as the loss of a child or a loss through suicide) you will start to move out of your "natural anesthesia," and you may actually experience a feeling of deeper pain. No one wants to hear this. However, this appears to be the natural course of grieving. You begin to realize the permanence of your loss at different levels.

Each time you reach another level, you may gasp and say, "Is this my reality now?" Just lean into this and be gentle with yourself. Be kind to yourself. If you have difficulty with the concept of self-care, it may take some practice to learn that this is not only okay but also necessary. Let this be a gift that comes out of this loss. You know what is said on an airplane: that you must put on your own oxygen mask before helping others. Self-Care does not mean Self-ish.

> **TRAVELER'S TIP**
> Be kind and gentle to yourself. Practice self-care daily.

There are days
I drop words
Of comfort on myself like
Falling
Leaves
And remember
That it is
Enough to be
Taken care of
By myself.

From Words of Comfort by Brian Andreas,
used with permission

of reality. When someone is in the despair of grief, they are in a most vulnerable and raw state. It takes courage to embrace that vulnerability, look at it head-on, and say, "This is who I was, this is who I am, and I will find out along the way (and with support) who I will become." If you or someone else expects you to be perfect or grieve in a certain way, resist that unrealistic expectation.

Please get professional counsel or read books about the damage that shame causes. It will take work and a willingness to be vulnerable and truthful, but imagine how freeing it will be to crawl out of the swamp. Shame is a heavy load to carry on top of the heaviness of grief. Listening to Brené Brown's TED Talk can teach you a lot about shame. She calls it the swampland of the soul.

There are many grievers who have made difficult decisions regarding end-of-life care. How many of us know the correct decisions? Even if you are trained in medicine, you may not know the "right" answer. We do the best we can with the knowledge that we have at that moment.

Second-guessing is often part of the grief process. What If's and If Only's will be looked at. "I should have" and "I could have" are often part of shame. But do not go to the extreme of blaming yourself or someone else for making a life or death decision and having that decision not go the way you wanted it to. How many decisions do we make every single day that could go one way or another? It is out of our hands. If I tell a friend directions to my house, and on the way, the friend gets rear-ended, is it my fault that I told her to go that way instead of going a different direction?

These kinds of scenarios play tricks on our minds, as if we have some control over the situations that occur. Don't buy into the illusion that we have control over life and death. We may do what we can to prepare and make good decisions, but in so many instances, the truth is that we do not have a lot of control.

> **TRAVELER'S TIP**
>
> Since shame goes so deep, you may need to get professional counseling to help with your distorted thoughts. A part of working through shame is to expose our vulnerabilities, as scary as that may sound. It takes finding the right person to trust. Do not let your secrets stay buried. You know the saying, "We are only as sick as our secrets." But since these thoughts are distorted, start by looking at the section on Stinkin' Thinkin'. Also, join a grief group. You may find that you are not alone in how you view your situation. You will find that it is easier to forgive others for the same thing you cannot forgive yourself for.

believing it will do you good. They do not realize that although it may be helpful for a little while, it may quickly become exhausting to put on the brave face.

This desert is not necessarily a bad place to be, and it may need to be crossed primarily by yourself. Reflect again on the metaphor of the butterfly in the cocoon. It is dark and lonely, but it also may have a feeling of safety. You must stay in this lonely cocoon until the metamorphosis takes place and your grief is transformed. You cannot open the cocoon too soon. Your healing and transformation must take the time that it needs. It can feel impossible right now, but it happens.

On the other hand, you must practice balance. If you feel that you are isolating too much and you are having difficulty functioning, then you need to get out and reconnect for a time, even if it is simply taking a walk in the fresh air.

> **TIP BOX**
> Find a balance between your safe cocoon and a community of understanding support.

FOREST FIRE
ANGER

I have no patience for stupid, uncaring people who don't understand what I'm going through. I could punch them. I'm angry at God. My faith is shaken. My loved one left me with a financial mess. We had plans to travel together! She should have taken better care of herself! My partner isn't grieving like I am. It feels like he doesn't care. I feel like yelling at the world, "Don't you realize I'm in pain???"

Sometimes people experience a constant level of irritability, and some experience flare-ups of anger. It is okay to allow yourself to experience all the emotions of grief. It is normal. Let them all in (remember the Rumi poem). Many do not experience anger initially or ever. That is okay too. The forest fire is not a place or stage that you must go through. Some people feel that they are betraying their loved one by feeling anger toward them. Remember that you have a right to feel how you feel (and the feeling will eventually pass and change).

113

Also, you may be in a place where nothing will comfort you and where you are just plain angry at the entire world.

RUGGED MOUNTAIN
BLAME

If only my sister would have taken better care of Mom. If only my family members wouldn't have been so greedy. If only the Living Trust would have been in place. The doctor never even read the chart. They ignored my requests.

Again, blaming is part of the process, but after a while—and often a long while—you will always arrive at the same destination: Your loved one is gone. It's a rugged mountain to climb, and blame can be a way of delaying your grief by not focusing on the depth of your sorrow. Many people stay stuck in the Blame Game. I have not seen that the outcome change by holding onto blame and anger. Anger is always a part of blame. And for most people, anger does not feel good. It gnaws at your stomach. In the end, you will have to practice forgiveness, so do it sooner rather than later.

BROKEN COMPASS
CONFUSION

What is my next step? I've lost my true North. I can't concentrate enough to pay a bill, let alone work on taxes or get a job! Grief makes me stupid! I can't seem to make the simplest decisions—paper or plastic? Who really cares? I don't know how this all happened or why. I can't make sense of what happened. I can't grasp this loss.

Sometimes grief upends a person. A person who was confident, intelligent, decisive, and efficient before their loss may now be floundering. This makes sense, though, because grief is complex and there are so many different things to process.

The "stages" of grief that were popularized in the past can further confuse people. Grievers may believe that they must go through a simplistic linear process—Denial, Anger, Bargaining, Depression, and finally "Ta Da!" Acceptance. They wonder "Why am I not angry?"

or "Why isn't 'Longing' listed on those stages because that is what I feel most of all?" or "Am I normal?" or "What is normal?" There may be phases, but there are no stages of grief.

It takes a long time to integrate your loss into your body and your mind. It takes quite a while for it to make sense, and this is especially so when the loss has been sudden and unexpected. Our minds seek completion. We need to make sense of things before our minds can rest. Our world needs to make sense. But when a death occurs, very often it does not make sense. Even if we were expecting it, we are surprised when our loved one takes his last breath.

Make sure that you are doing proper self-care so that your brain can function as well as possible. Even if you are taking care of yourself, the swirling emotions will feel confusing for a while. Some people call it brain fog. It is normal. It will pass.

Also, putting structure into your daily life and on your calendar is very helpful. Schedule something that you can look forward to. It's okay to struggle with the world not making sense. It's okay to let your compass be broken for a while. Do this for as long as you need to in order to let it be. It is better to let this happen naturally rather than forcing it. And at some point, even several years down the road, if you are still haunted by it not making sense, then do some EMDR or expressive arts to nudge the confusion along. Eventually you may have to be okay with the knowledge that life has many mysteries that may not be revealed on this physical plane.

TRAVELER'S TIP

Rest assured that this is a temporary state and your brain will eventually function the way it used to. It is normal to a point. If after years you are still fretting about things not making sense, then seek professional help. Also realize that life and the universe hold many mysteries that are not always explainable. Do not drive yourself to despair asking, "Why?" Let it be.

TRAVELER'S TALE

"When my seventeen-year-old son took his own life, it was like all the pieces of the puzzle of my life blew up in the air. I scrambled to put the pieces back. I drove myself crazy wondering how I could have missed the signs. I even went back to remembering when he was in the womb and I dropped a pair of scissors. He jumped. I should have realized then how sensitive he was. I realize now that there will always be some pieces of the puzzle missing. I know I was a good and loving mom. It has taken a long time, but I've forgiven myself, and I'm at peace. I still miss him though."

FIELD OF FLOWERS
RELIEF

This has been a long, painful journey, and I'm glad it is over. Is that bad? My life has been difficult and empty for so long, and now I feel a weight has lifted off me. My loved one struggled for so many years with depression and addiction, and I was always worried about his safety. At least now the worrying has stopped. I must be a heartless person. This is a confusing time for me.

Relief comes in all different forms and may not apply to everyone. Relief can be unique to those who have had a long struggle with their loved one, such as those who suffered from addictions or severe mental health issues. Often these grievers have lived in constant fear of a phone call that delivers dreaded news. A person who has been a caregiver for months or years knows the extreme toll that it takes emotionally and physically watching your loved one deteriorate in health and dignity. Sometimes relief is that the loved one is no longer in pain or that the caregiver can finally rest after the exhaustion of being on-call 24/7. Resting in this field of flowers may produce guilt or confusion. Allow all these feelings and know that they are normal. Relief will undoubtedly change as time goes on. Like the facets of a prism, each feeling will present itself for you to look at. Allow the rest for a time because at some point, more complex feelings will occur that you will have to wrestle with.

TRAVELER'S TALE

"For the first few months when I attended Widows' Group, I could not relate to the sorrow of the other members. For me, after taking care of my husband who had Parkinson's for over a decade, I felt lighter than I had in years. But when the relief dissipated, I reflected on our long married life. We were happy for most of those years. The sorrow of losing that life trumped any feelings of relief. I also learned that it's okay to feel relief and sadness at the same time. The two are not mutually exclusive."

TRAVELER'S TIP

Relief can be a normal reaction initially. It's okay to relax in this until the other facets present themselves for inspection.

PART FIVE: WHAT'S IN YOUR BACKPACK

You have hopefully picked up many tools to put in your Backpack. Pick and choose which tools work for you. Choose several or choose the whole list. Then practice, practice, practice. This is what is meant by doing the grief work. Processing or working through your grief does not just mean speaking to a counselor, reading a book, or going to a support group. It means all this and more if you want to move down Courage Road with as few bumps and scars as possible.

> All these tools help to integrate your loss, not to "get over" it. And with integration comes new meaning to life. The hope is that you will eventually heal and live a new life, a life that you perhaps had never thought about or thought possible.

terfly takes place in the cocoon. Find your safe place either physically or metaphorically to grieve the way you need to. Emerge from the cocoon when you have done your grief work and when the time is right for you.

Connect the Dots—Often grievers wonder why they are so exhausted or particularly fragile this week or month. Most people minimize their loss because our culture is not comfortable embracing grief. So remind yourself that you have had a blow to your psyche. Also, how long has it been since your loved one died? One month, three months, six? Each month will have a different feel to it. Remember that often (most of the time), your grief will get harder before it eases up. Is it the month of a special birthday or anniversary? Connect these dots to understand where you are on the grief map.

Courage—If you have read this far, then you already have the courage that it takes to face the pain, do the work, honor your loved one, and be open to new beginnings. Good for you.

Compassion—Learn to develop compassion for yourself instead of self-pity. Think about how you would want to comfort a friend who is grieving; now do this for yourself.

Dive through the Grief Waves—An essential concept to help you move through the pain (or wave) instead of running from it. It will pass; it always does.

Distract—Sometimes you just need to take a break from all the emotions. Watch a movie that is geared toward kids—Disney or Pixar movies. They usually have good messages and are uplifting.

Eat well—Food can taste like cardboard during this difficult time, and what tastes best is comfort food. Be aware of mindless eating. Eat as healthily as you can so your brain functions properly. You may have a lot of decisions to make, therefore a clear brain is needed. Try drinking healthy smoothies with lots of greens.

EMDR—Short-term treatment to help process trauma. I call it a magic wand. It is amazingly effective, but does not replace doing your grief work. Also, check into

EFT—Emotional Freedom Technique—which involves tapping.

Empathy—Remember that you have not walked in another's shoes, and they have not walked in yours. Be gentle in thought and deed with yourself and with others.

Forgiveness—Look at ways you are holding on to unforgiveness. This will damage you in many ways. Recommended books in Resources.

of "BUT." This is a subtle shift that seems to help. Try it.

Permission—Give yourself permission to grieve the way you need to without judgment or undue influence. Don't minimize what you are feeling. You have a right to your feelings.

Perseverance—Courage Road may be long, but you cannot quit. Just take it one step at a time.

Perspective—When you are in the midst of deep grief, your frame of reference will be dark and narrow and perhaps dismal. Keep in mind that you do not yet have a broad view of possibilities. I urge you to get off your "island" and take a trip, even to the other side of town. Widen your view, broaden your horizon. You will not see a panorama now, but trust that in time you might. As you travel further down the Road, be sure to look back and note any lessons learned or strengths gained from using the tools in your Backpack.

Practice—Practice changing up your routines; practice taking items out of the house; practice venturing out of the house; practice living until you are alive again.

Reflect—On how grief has been occurring since the beginning of time. Connect with and say a prayer for all those people who are experiencing deep loss and trauma daily in your community. Then expand those thoughts and prayers to the people in your state, your nation, the world.

Scrapbook—The process of going through photos, including poetry or meaningful quotes, is healing. Take your time doing this. Shed tears and breathe.

Self-Care—This is part of having compassion for yourself. What would you tell a friend to do for his or herself if they were in deep grief? Do this for yourself. Make a daily list of three things that you can do to take care of yourself. Practice doing at least one each day. When you go into an intense downward loop, look at the list as a reminder of how to be kind to yourself. Many of the tools on this list can be considered self-care, but there are also numerous books on the subject. Remember that self-care does not mean self-ish.

Self Talk—"I can make it through this." "I must trust the healing process." "I'll keep my heart and mind open to whatever unfolds along the journey." Use what fits for you.

Shoulds—This is a cognitive distortion or part of the list of Stinkin' Thinkin' (see Appendix) but deserves a place on the tool list to remind you not to "should" on yourself. What purpose will this serve? Absolutely none.

is not a solution to "get over" it. Try not to burn out your friendships. Some friends have the ability to listen for as long as you need. Others will be there to distract you when you need a break from grieving. And others know how to take action and do for you. Be aware of the unique gifts that they offer as well as those they cannot. Gather your support system around you like a comforting blanket.

Teflon Mind Trick—If people are making insensitive but well-meaning comments, or if they are stirring up drama and throwing bombs your way, then attempt to let them roll off the top of your head. Just like a Teflon (or non-stick) pan, whatever is cooked in it slides right off. Picture this when a comment gets thrown your way. Don't let it stick.

Tell a New Story—If you are stuck in a relentless script, rehashing the same events, then it's time (after a period) to tell a new, more positive story. Even if you do not believe your new story at first, imagine life with this shift in thinking.

Triggers—A trigger can be anything that initiates or precipitates a reaction, usually a negative one. These can happen out of the blue and throw you into a down loop. For example, going past a special restaurant or seeing a similar car drive by. If the same triggers keep occurring, can some of these triggers be avoided until you can handle them better? If not, remember that the down loop will not send you to the bottom. Trust that in time you will accommodate to these triggers.

Trust—Trust the healing process and that you will have a shift over time.

Up Loops—Use them wisely. During an up loop, be aware of the little strengths and insights that you gain. Each up loop is a testament to your endurance. Savor the feeling that you feel when an up loop occurs. Savoring it actually changes your brain chemistry. Also, take advantage of the energy to accomplish some tasks. Inevitably a down loop will occur.

Weigh the Pros and Cons—If you are struggling with a decision, sit down and write a list of the pros and cons. Seeing it on paper helps declutter your mind.

Write—A letter to your loved one if there is any unfinished business that needs to be addressed. Then write a letter from your loved one to you. Imagine what your loved one would say in response to your letter. Pay attention to what is going on with you as you write the letters. It's the process of doing this exercise that is important, not the product.

often may not even remember the words I say to guide them through. They just remember the foundation and structure of a person they trust to be there.

Please note that "Further down the Road" is your own time frame. This could mean four months, one year, or five. You need to have your own definition of what it means to heal. Further down the road may mean that you are thinking less about the circumstances of the death and more about the impact of your life without your loved one. What will your future look like without the one who was the first to say Happy Birthday or the one with whom you shared the biggest laughs or the one who just "got" you. You may still be shaking your head in disbelief, but less often.

Life's questions, going deeper, expanding long-held beliefs about yourself and the world, may surface at this point. This is a good thing, and it may also be frightening. Notice the conjunctive And instead of But. It is useful to start holding two ideas side by side instead of opposing one another. It's a subtle distinction but worth exploring. (See What's In Your Backpack: Paradoxical Statements).

One of my clients asked me, "What is the purpose of grief?" I said that it is perhaps a measure stick to show how much you love that person. You know, you can't have the light without the dark. She responded emphatically, "I don't need this much pain to tell me how much I love him. I already know!"

I guess the end result of all the pain of grief is that you want it to count for something. You do not want to go through all the heart-wrenching terrain, do all the grief work, see light at the end of the Road, just to have it mean nothing. That would be superficial. It is similar to the people who survive cancer without changing anything emotionally, physically, or spiritually in their lives. You want to bop them on the head and ask, "Didn't you learn anything through this ordeal?"

What most of my clients say that they learned, at the very least, is compassion for other grievers. Until one has been through it, one does not know how to support a griever. You can't know what you don't know, right?

As you go further down the Road, the Loops, Waves, or Grief Bombs will start coming further apart. That means that you will "be okay" for longer periods of time, gaining more strengths and insights and having less periods of despair. You may begin to have more periods of lightness. You may venture out more, make more plans, think about more possibilities.

But be prepared, because undoubtedly you will hit

another grief bomb, and it may be extremely intense. It may throw you back to where you *feel* that you are at the bottom again. Remember, however, that you are not at the bottom. The intensity is there because you had a longer period of "okay," and you became comfortable, whistling down the Road thinking that the pain was behind you. Then *Slam!* These Grief Bombs may occur for no reason, or they may occur as you approach an anniversary or birthday or event. They may occur when you run across a letter in your loved one's handwriting. Although intense, hopefully the duration will be shorter. You have hopefully been practicing the tools that will get you through a down loop more smoothly. And keep in mind that this is still *normal*.

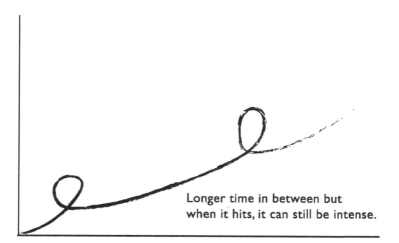

Longer time in between but when it hits, it can still be intense.

Loops of Recovery Further Down the Road

At this point, you may ask yourself where on the Road are you feeling stuck. What terrain, if any, keeps popping onto your path? Hopefully, time will have given you some perspective and that many of the emotions such as guilt or fear will have started to resolve. If not, do your grief work. Remember the buffet approach to healing.

If what you have been doing is no longer working, then do something else. If the tools that have helped you are no longer helping, try something else. And try using different sides of your brain. This is an important element that can help you dislodge what is stuck. Something new may be revealed in a way that opens you to new horizons. It can be exciting, daunting, perplexing, scary, and engrossing all at once.

Remember the beehive that was in front of your face with all the emotions of grief? That was super exhausting. These *new* emotions can be exhilarating. I do not mean it in the sense of being cheerful or merry, but more like feeling like new buds in springtime. There may be a glimpse that life will not always be dark and dreary. You may entertain the possibility that new life, albeit a different life, can begin. One client said, "I don't have joy yet, but I can en-joy certain things about my life now." Begin to look for the things in life that you can enjoy.

DUCK WALKING ON TWO PARALLEL ROADS

At this point, let's look at two parallel Roads. The first is Courage Road. You have been travelling on it for a long time. You have been doing your grief work, running into side paths, detours, and the many different types of terrain. At some point, a parallel road comes into your life. It may have a bit more sunlight on it, not so shaded by thick trees or prickly cactus.

There may be more Vista Points where you can look back at where you have been travelling. You might reflect on some new perspective that you did not think you could have arrived at when you started the first steps on Courage Road. From these Vista Points, you might also acknowledge that your loss does not consume every moment and that you are beginning to see more color.

In my office, I would often observe this point in time because my clients would ask, "Did you get a new painting?" This was a big colorful painting directly in their view behind me. I would tell them that it has been there the whole time. Their response was amusement or disbelief. It meant that they were opening up to color. You might say to yourself, "Well, if I'm going to live without my loved one, I might as well begin to see what living means for me." You might toy with the idea of becoming more sociable, reconnecting with friendships that you let go during the darker days of grief. Perhaps you will explore altogether new avenues of friendship. As your body begins to thaw, then your heart will open ever so slightly.

On this new Road, you may intentionally explore a new hobby, new beliefs, or seek new opportunities. One client took up photography as a hobby. She expressed that looking through the lens made the raw world a bit softer.

Because the two Roads are parallel, you may feel that you are duck walking—one foot on each Road at times, or perhaps rabbit hopping from one Road to the other and then back again. Whereas on the first road you were walking in a fog or robotically stepping one foot in front of the other, now begin to make your steps more intentional, more purposeful.

> ### 👥 TRAVELER'S TALE
>
> "When my dad died, I was devastated. I wanted to honor him in a way that I hoped would make him proud. He was an excellent cook and also a musician. I decided to take cooking lessons and guitar lessons. At first, I was enthusiastic. After several months, however, I realized that these were his passions, not mine. I realized that my dad would want me to find my own direction."

You may want to explore what you wish to take from your "old" life into your "new" life and what you want to leave behind.

Remember the cocoon that kept you safe? That cocoon may begin to feel a bit cramped, perhaps even gloomy. When you are ready, and only then, let the butterfly emerge from its metamorphoses. Evolution happens. Life continues. Allow it.

PART SEVEN: THE CHAPTER YOU WRITE YOURSELF

There is no final destination, no stepping off point. You have been on a journey and the journey has been a process. As we know, life is a process and this is what you will continue to write.

You are a different person now, and hopefully one who has gained compassion and insight and other "gifts" as a result of your loss. You will never stop missing your loved one, but the pain will soften. A griever said after several years down the Road, "I remember the pain, but I no longer *feel* the pain."

Let the loss of your loved one have some purpose in your life. At least you now know how to be there for someone who has had a recent loss. This alone is significant.

I wish you well on your continued journey. Thank you for having the courage to walk down Courage Road.

You are not alone.

APPENDIX

PART 1: LOOPS OF RECOVERY INFOGRAPHIC

The following page is an important piece of information about how the healing process goes. Remember that healing is not a straight line upward. When you start to go upward that feels good, but be aware that there will be a downward loop. The down loop makes you *feel* that you are starting at Rock Bottom. This is not true because Feeling Pass and Feelings Change. Trust the healing process.

3. Blaming—You blame yourself for something you were not entirely responsible for, or you blame others overlooking ways that your own attitudes and behavior may contribute to a problem. This kind of distortion produces anger that is physically and emotionally harmful to your health. Although you may have a right to your feelings, be careful how you express it.

4. WWPT—What Will People Think? You are more worried about keeping up appearances than being authentic. Keeping up a façade is exhausting.

5. Being Right—You feel that you are on trial to prove to everyone you are right; you constantly defend yourself. Ask yourself whether it is more important to be right or be at peace.

6. Fallacy of Fairness—You believe that everything in life has to be fair. We know this is simply not true, even if this is something we value and want. Fairness is subjective. What is fair to one person may not be fair to another.

7. Fallacy of Change—You have no control over changing others. You can only change yourself in the situation.

8. Fallacy of Control—You believe that if you exercise control over a situation the outcome will be okay or different. Situations about life and death are usually much bigger than us being able to wield control over them.

9. Magnification or Minimization—You blow things out of proportion or you minimize important things. Be aware of how these can make situations worse.

10. What If's and If Only's—You drive yourself crazy thinking about these without getting any concrete answers. Also, "Why's" are not very productive in the long run. These produce anxiety. Our mind naturally seeks completion and answers.

It is okay to wrestle with these for a while, but at some point, when the wrestling becomes tedious, then it's okay to let it be.

11. Terminal Uniqueness—You believe that no one understands you and that your situation is unique, therefore, you may isolate or not listen to suggestions. Holding firm on these beliefs may result in you being bitter and alone.

12. Should Statements—You criticize yourself or others with "Shoulds" or "Shouldn'ts." "Musts," "Oughts," and "Have tos" are similar offenders. Don't SHOULD on yourself or others.

13. Emotional Reasoning—You reason from how you feel at the time. Example: "I'm a failure." "I'm stupid." Remember that feelings are just feelings. They are neither right nor wrong. They change, they pass, and they can lie. Separate who you are from what you feel.

14. Past-Tripping—You are stuck thinking about the past. Thinking about the past is normal. But when you are stuck on a particular scene, then it may be time to get extra help.

15. Future-Tripping—You constantly worry about what will happen in the future, which creates anxiety and fear. Most future things that one worries about never come true. Make a list so it is on paper and not bouncing around in your head. Also, try to stay in the present. Day-trip instead of future-trip.

16. Jumping to Conclusions or Catastrophizing—You make something worse than it is without weighing the evidence. This is similar to Future-Tripping and it can become paralyzing. On paper, weigh the evidence for and against. Seek help around these issues.

17. Labeling—You identify with your shortcomings or label others arbitrarily. "I'm an idiot. I'm doing everything wrong." "They are all incompetent." Realize that everyone makes mistakes, no one is perfect, and most people are doing the best they can. Labeling yourself or others just stirs the Stinkin' Thinkin' pot.

18. Heaven's Reward Fallacy—You believe that if you just work hard and do "what's right" then things will turn out. This belief may work in life, but is a myth when it comes to death, dying, and grieving. Try to be positive and realistic at the same time.

PART 3: HOW TO USE THE 4-COLUMN TECHNIQUE

STEP 1. The first column is labeled Automatic Negative Thoughts. These thoughts may not necessarily be negative. For grievers, these thoughts may be normal. But they are the ones that may be keeping you from moving along Courage Road. Notice which thoughts repeatedly nag in your mind and write them down.

If there is something you can do about it, then do it. More often than not, however, the thoughts are not serving a purpose. They may be beating you up unnecessarily. So go to Step #2.

STEP 2. This column stops the runaway train from rolling down the tracks. Say "STOP! WHAT IS IT GOOD FOR? ABSOLUTELY NOTHING!" You will remember this by the tune of "War" by Edwin Starr.

Whatever your automatic thought is, if it just keeps picking at you, you need to stop it. Does it serve a purpose? Usually not. Then you must go on to the next two steps. If you don't, then that train will just keep rolling.

STEP 3. Identify the Distortion. Take your checklist of Stinkin' Thinkin' and see which Automatic Thought fits best with the list. Several may apply. It could be All or Nothing Thinking and Magnification. Identifying what applies helps you become very familiar with the list. You will soon begin to recognize when you are using Stinkin' Thinkin', thus stirring a pot that is better left still.

THE 4-COLUMN TECHNIQUE

Automatic Negative Thought	STOP! What is it good for? Absolutely Nothing!
I will never get over this. I am broken.	STOP!
My sister never helped when mom needed the help. I did everything! She should have helped more. It's not fair.	STOP! This is just fueling my anger.
I'm just not a Support Group kind of person. I don't want to listen to others' pain. I have enough of my own. Anyway, no one can relate to what I've gone through.	STOP!

STEP 4. This step is essential to rewiring your faulty thinking. Replace the automatic thought that is bothering you with something healthier, even if you do not believe it one hundred percent at the moment. If you cannot come up with anything that resonates, then think about what you would say to a friend, or find someone who can help. Then, focus more on column four than your Automatic Thoughts.

Identify the Distortion	Replace with Healthier Thought
Black & White Thinking	Some day I may heal, but I will always miss my loved one. I feel broken now, but this intense feeling may pass.
Black & White Filtering Blaming Shoulding Fallacy of Fairness	My sister helped when she could. After all, she lived in another state. I need to work on letting these feelings be because I don't want to ruin a relationship.
Terminal Uniqueness	Maybe it will help and maybe it won't. I need to keep an open mind. I can give it a try.

PART 4: WHAT YOUR LOVED ONES CAN EXPECT

People who love you and want to support you during your bereavement often don't know how to help or what to say to be of comfort. And sometimes, with the best of intentions, they can even make you feel worse!

Here is a valuable list of things your family and friends should understand about the normal bereavement process so they can help you more effectively and worry less about you. Please make copies to give to the people who love you.

- My grief process will take much longer than you (or I) want it to.
- You can't fix my pain for me by doing anything, but I really appreciate you just being there for me.
- I will be in a sort of fog for at least three months. When the fog lifts, I might actually seem worse.
- I will have periods of doing okay, then I will feel despair again.
- I will be exhausted. Grieving is hard work.
- My desire, creativity, and motivation will be gone for quite a while.
- My ability to experience joy may also be absent.
- I may have a range of emotions, from irritability to inexplicable rage, and it may be targeted at you. Please forgive me.
- I am vulnerable, I feel brittle, and I do not feel resilient or competent.
- I can't take too much stimulation. I probably won't feel like being sociable.
- I know you miss the old me, but I'm forever changed by the loss of my loved one.
- It will feel as though I haven't made any progress. However, I am slowly healing with occasional normal setbacks. I will heal. Please be patient, loving, and understanding.

PART 5: ASSERTIVENESS BILL OF RIGHTS

Every man and woman has the following basic human rights:

- The right to refuse requests without having to feel guilty or selfish.
- The right to express anger appropriately.
- The right to make mistakes.
- The right to have your opinions given the same respect and consideration that other people's opinions are given.
- The right to have your needs be as important as the needs of other people.
- The right to be independent.
- The right not to be codependent.
- The right not to justify your behavior. "No." is complete sentence.
- The right to change your mind.
- The right to say "I don't know" or "I need to think about it."
- The right to decide if you are responsible for solving other people's problems. Helping does not always help.
- The right not to understand. The right not to always have answers.
- The right not to care.

You may choose not to exercise all or even one of these rights at any given time. You can exercise some of them some of the time or all of them all of the time. This is your decision, not one that can be forced on you by someone else.

RESOURCES

These are some books that I recommend.

Tear Soup: A Recipe for Healing After Loss by Pat Schwiebert and Chuck DeKlyen. Illustrated by Taylor Bills

The Artist's Way: A Spiritual Path to Higher Creativity by Julia Cameron

Forgive for Good: A Proven Prescription for Health and Happiness by Frederic Luskin

The Book of Forgiving: The Fourfold Path for Healing Ourselves and Our World by Desmond Tutu

On Living by Kerry Egans

Healing After Loss: Daily Meditations For Working Through Grief by Martha Whitmore Hickman

Ambiguous Loss: Learning to Live with Unresolved Grief by Pauline Boss

The Little Book of Gratitude by Robert A. Emmons

In the Sea of Grief and Love by Susan Cochran

Nurturing Healing Love: A Mother's Journey of Hope and Forgiveness by Scarlett Lewis

Dying to Be Free: A Healing Guide for Families after a Suicide by Beverly Cobain and Jean Larch

Every Last One by Anna Quindlen

Yoga for Grief Relief by Antonio Sausys

Swimming in the Sink: An Episode of the Heart by Lynne Cox

CPSIA information can be obtained
at www.ICGtesting.com
Printed in the USA
FSOW04n1446121117
40862FS